# The Last Straw

# The Last Straw

A *For Better or For Worse*
Collection by Lynn Johnston

Foreword by Charles M. Schulz

**Andrews, McMeel & Parker**
A Universal Press Syndicate Company
Kansas City ● New York

Foreword

The comic pages needed Lynn Johnston. They needed someone with her distinctive approach.

I have noticed lately that a lot of the so-called gags in some of our newer strips are virtually interchangeable. Not Lynn's. Her ideas match her characters. She can draw, too. She can draw telephones, dentists' chairs, fat ladies, skinny ladies, dogs, trumpets, kids, and dresser drawers. She also can coin phrases like "leftunders" for "leftovers." And she isn't afraid of sadness, as when Lizzie became ill.

The comic pages needed Lynn Johnston — and she arrived just in time.

CHARLES M. SCHULZ
Creator of Peanuts

WHAT ARE YOU DOING IN THE CRAWL SPACE, MOM?

LOOKING FOR STUFF TO SELL AT THE YARD SALE.

YOU CAN'T SELL THIS! IT'S MY VERY FAVORITE THING IN THE WHOLE WORLD!!

WHAT IS IT?

THIS IS ALL THE STUFF I'VE COLLECTED THAT WE NEVER USE.

ELLY—THAT'S MY DUFFEL COAT! YOU CAN'T SELL MY DUFFEL COAT!

I HAVEN'T WORN IT BECAUSE I'M WAITING FOR THE STYLE TO COME BACK!

JOHN ... YOU WON'T LIVE THAT LONG!!!

WHY IS IT THAT WHEN I DECIDE TO SELL SOMETHING IT BECOMES TOO PRECIOUS TO PART WITH?

WE HAVE LOADS OF JUST PLAIN JUNK THAT NOBODY USES, WEARS OR PLAYS WITH!!

HEY! LET'S CHUCK OUT THIS HIDEOUS WALL CLOCK!

ARE YOU KIDDING? MY MOTHER GAVE ME THAT!!!

HEY, MAN! WHAT'S HAPPENING?

MOM'S HAVIN' A YARD SALE.

THE PEOPLE SHE WORKS WITH HAVE ALL BROUGHT THEIR JUNK OVER TO OUR PLACE.

YEAH? WHEN ARE THEY GONNA START THE SALE?

I DUNNO.

THEY'RE STILL BUYING JUNK FROM EACH OTHER.

OK, I'LL GIVE YOU THIS FOR $2. IF YOU TAKE THE SPOONS AS WELL...

WHERE HAVE ALL THESE PEOPLE COME FROM? SOME I'VE NEVER SEEN IN MY LIFE!

EASTGATE LIBRARY YARD SALE

I GO EFF'RY YARD SALE IN CITY—AN' I GIFF YOU THE 6 OUTA 10 FOR DIS VON.

NO REFRESHMENTS.

WE'RE RUNNING OUT OF STUFF, ELLY, AND THE SALE DOESN'T END FOR ANOTHER HOUR!

EASTGATE LIBRARY YARD SALE

WAIT! I'LL RUN INTO THE HOUSE AND FIND SOME MORE JUNK!

WHAT DO YOU MEAN—TAKE OFF THESE PANTS?!!!

ONE-HALF HOUR TO GO— WE ARE SLASHING OUR PRICES, EVERYBODY!

EVERYTHING 50% OFF— DON'T MISS THESE BARGAINS! YARD SALE

¡WHEW¿ THAT'S IT! WE DID IT. WE SOLD NEARLY THE WHOLE WORKS!

MOM?....HAS ANYONE SEEN MY BICYCLE?

SO NOW THAT THE CRAZINESS IS OVER, YOU CAN COUNT YOUR PENNIES.

PENNIES? JOHN, WE MADE OVER $800 ON THAT YARD SALE!

SOME IDIOT EVEN PAID $25 FOR OUR OLD BLACK-AND-WHITE TV!

....I THOUGHT IT LOOKED FAMILIAR.

WELL, YOU CERTAINLY CLEARED OUT THE HOUSE, EL!

GETTING RID OF ALL OUR JUNK HAS GIVEN US A LOT MORE STORAGE SPACE!

WHAT ARE WE GOING TO DO WITH ALL THIS ROOM?

FILL IT WITH MORE JUNK!

HOW'S LIZZIE, MOM?

STILL NOT WELL, MIKE.

I WANNA SEE HER.

SHE'S ASLEEP.

DUMB GERMS!

YOUR MOM'S TAKEN LIZZIE TO THE HOSPITAL.

HOW COME?

HER FEVER IS WORSE AND WE WERE WORRIED.

IT'S OK, MICHAEL. GO BACK TO BED. LIZZIE WILL BE JUST FINE.

PROMISE?

THEY'RE KEEPING LIZZIE IN THE HOSPITAL OVERNIGHT FOR OBSERVATION.

SHE IS SO SICK, JOHN.... AND I FEEL SO GUILTY!

THINGS LIKE THIS JUST HAPPEN, ELLY. WHY SHOULD YOU FEEL SO GUILTY?

I YELLED AT HER YESTERDAY!

I KNOW THAT SHE'S PROBABLY GOING TO BE FINE...

BUT LOOKING AT LIZZIE'S EMPTY BED MAKES ME FEEL AWFUL INSIDE.

WHAT'S THE MATTER, JOHN? WHAT WERE YOU DOING?

IMAGINING THE UNIMAGINABLE.

IT'S THE DOCTOR, JOHN. THEY'RE PUTTING ELIZABETH ON INTRAVENOUS MEDICATION!

WHERE ARE YOU GOING?

TO THE HOSPITAL.

IF I'M NOT GOING TO SLEEP — I MIGHT AS WELL NOT SLEEP THERE!

GOOD MORNING, MRS. PATTERSON. CAN I GET YOU A CUP OF COFFEE?

YOU CAN SEE ELIZABETH. SHE'S JUST WAKING UP!

IS SHE OK? IS SHE GOING TO BE ALL RIGHT?

HI, MOM!!

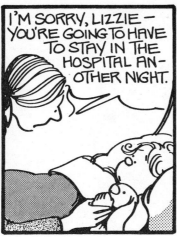

I'M TELLING YOU, ANNE... WITH LIZZIE STILL SICK I FIND STAYING HOME A REAL CHORE.

BEFORE I GOT MY JOB, I DON'T KNOW WHAT I DID TO PRESERVE MY SANITY!

YOU HAD COFFEE WITH ME.

BEFORE YOU STARTED WORKING I USED TO SEE YOU NEARLY EVERY DAY.

WE'D GET TOGETHER... HAVE A COFFEE... TALK ABOUT THINGS...

NOW I JUST SEE YOU ONCE IN A WHILE.

I MISS YOU, EL.

I THINK I'LL LET LIZ GO BACK TO PLAYCARE TOMORROW, ANNIE. SHE'S BETTER NOW.

STILL I'D HATE TO LET HER SPREAD THAT VIRUS AROUND THE DAY CARE CENTER!

WHY WORRY?

IT'S PROBABLY WHERE SHE PICKED IT UP IN THE FIRST PLACE!

IT'S GOOD TO SEE YOU BACK AT WORK, ELLY!

WE'VE LEFT THE SUMMER READING CONTESTS AND THE WINDOW DISPLAYS FOR YOU TO DO...

I'M AFRAID WE LET A LOT OF THINGS PILE UP ON YOUR DESK.

THEY MISSED ME!!

MY MOM CALLED THE SCHOOL. SHE'S GONNA BE LATE HOME FROM WORK TODAY.

SHE SAYS I GOTTA GO OVER TO THAT DUMB ANNIE'S AN' WAIT FOR HER.

HOW COME SHE WON'T GIVE ME A KEY TO THE HOUSE? THAT'S WHAT I WANNA KNOW!

YEAH! YOU, ME AN' THE GUYS WOULD LOOK AFTER IT!

UGH. MOM 'XPECTS ME TO GO PLAY WITH THAT DUMB CHRISTOPHER AN' HIS BABY BROTHER.

WELL, NOTHING IN THIS WORLD IS GONNA GET ME INTO THAT HOUSE!

I'LL STAY OUT IN THEIR YARD AN' WAIT FOR MY MOM, BUT I WON'T GO INSIDE.

UNLESS.... IT RAINS....

21

SO—MICHAEL TOLD YOU THAT HE DIDN'T LIKE ME WORKING, DID HE. ..JOHN...WE'VE BEEN THROUGH ALL THIS!!

LIZ IS IN DAY CARE, MIKE IS IN SCHOOL... WHY SHOULD I STAY HOME WHEN EVERYONE ELSE IS AWAY?!

WHAT AM I SUPPOSED TO DO ALL DAY—BAKE COOKIES?!! DUST ARMCHAIRS?!!

FROM NOW ON... MICHAEL FIGHTS HIS OWN BATTLES.

KNOW WHAT WE SHOULD DO, ELLY? SEND MIKE TO VANCOUVER!

HE'S OLD ENOUGH TO TRAVEL ON HIS OWN.

WE COULD PUT HIM ON THE PLANE AT THIS END...AND YOUR MOM COULD PICK HIM UP AT THE OTHER.

YOU MUSTA DONE SOMETHIN' REAL BAD, MICHAEL—THEY'RE TALKING 'BOUT SENDIN' YOU AWAY!

GOIN' ON A PLANE ALL BY YOURSELF! FAR OUT, MAN!

MY MOM CALLED MY GRANDMA AN' SHE SAID SHE'D MEET ME WHEN I GET OFF.

WOW! MOST GUYS DON'T GET TO DO THAT 'TILL THEY'RE GROWN UP!

YEAH. I KNOW.

BEFORE YOU GO, I WANT TO FIND YOU SOME NICE TRAVELING CLOTHES.

WE DON'T WANT GRANDMA TO SEE YOU GETTING OFF THE PLANE LOOKING LIKE THAT!

YOU'LL BE A CLEAN AND TIDY YOUNG GENTLEMAN FOR A CHANGE.

THEN HOW'S SHE GONNA KNOW IT'S ME

STAND UP STRAIGHT! PUT YOUR ARMS DOWN. STOP SCRATCHING!!

HOW AM I GOING TO SEE IF THESE FIT IF YOU DON'T STAND STILL!

ANYTHING I CAN DO TO HELP YOU IN THERE?

YES—HAVE YOU GOT ANYTHING IN A STRAITJACKET? SIZE 12?

DO YOU REALLY THINK WE'RE DOING THE RIGHT THING — SENDING MICHAEL ON A PLANE ALL BY HIMSELF?

SURE. HE'S A BIG BOY. HE'LL BE ABLE TO HANDLE IT JUST FINE!

YEAH.

···BUT···· I DON'T THINK I WILL.

IT WASN'T MUCH OF A MEAL, PHIL.

THAT'S OK, SIS.

MIND IF I HAVE A CIGARETTE?

HOW COME, WHEN YOU STAY HERE FOR SUPPER YOU ALWAYS GOTTA HAVE A CIGARETTE AFTER?

IT KILLS THE TASTE.

UNCLE PHIL... IF I ASK YOU A VERY PRIVATE QUESTION, WILL YOU PROMISE NOT TO TELL?

IT'S IMPORTANT. IT'S A DECISION THAT COULD CHANGE MY WHOLE LIFE!

WHEN I GO... BY MYSELF ... ON THE PLANE — TO SEE MY GRANDMA FOR TWO WHOLE WEEKS....

SHOULD I TAKE MY TEDDY?

I KNOW HOW IMPORTANT YOUR TEDDY IS TO YOU, MAN. I HAD ONE ONCE — EVEN HAD A SECURITY BLANKET!

WOW.

THEN, ONE DAY — SOMETHING CAME INTO MY LIFE... AND I HAD TO GIVE THEM UP.

I KNOW WHAT IT WAS — GIRLS!! RIGHT?

NOPE. ...SCOUT CAMP.

**WE'LL BE PREBOARDING YOU IN A MINUTE, MICHAEL.**

**UH- EXCUSE ME ...**

**I KNOW THE "M" MEANS "MINOR" ON THIS TAG- BUT WHAT DOES THE "U" STAND FOR?**

**UNACCOMPANIED.**

**GOOD. DADDY SAID IT WAS FOR "UNTRAINED."**

**COULD YOU TELL ME HOW LONG IT WILL TAKE TO GET TO VANCOUVER PLEASE?**

**WE LAND IN CALGARY- SO IT'LL BE ANOTHER 3 HOURS AT LEAST, MICHAEL.**

**GOSH. I SURE WISH I'D BROUGHT MORE TO PLAY WITH!!**

**STOP FIDGETING, ELLY! MICHAEL'S ON HIS WAY AND HE'LL BE JUST FINE.**

**HE'S GOT BOOKS, TOYS, — HE'LL GET PLENTY OF ATTENTION.**

**THERE'S NOTHING TO WORRY ABOUT.**

**CLICK!**

**FURTHER INVESTIGATION INTO THE FATAL CRASH OF A 737 PASSENGER JET HAS REVEALED THAT....**

DID YOU TAKE MOM AN' UNCLE PHIL FISHING WHEN THEY WERE LITTLE?

OH, SURE. BUT I DIDN'T HAVE MUCH TIME THEN. NOT MUCH MONEY, EITHER.

...NOW I'VE GOT ME A BOAT AND PLENTY OF TIME... BUT ELLY AND PHIL ARE GROWN AND GONE.

LIFE SOMETIMES WORKS BACKWARD..... DOESN'T IT, GRAMPA.

YESSIR—I CAN SEE THESE BABIES NOW... FRIED IN BUTTER— JUST WAITING FOR US TO SINK OUR TEETH INTO 'EM!

YEAH! I WONDER WHAT GRANDMA WILL SAY WHEN SHE SEES THEM!

YOU CAUGHT 'EM— YOU CLEAN 'EM!!

ON SECOND THOUGHT... THEY'D BE GOOD FOR THE GARDEN.

SEE? CLEANING A FISH IS NO PROBLEM.

SLIT 'ER OPEN, EMPTY 'ER OUT... CHOP 'ER HERE, SCALE 'ER LIKE THIS...

THERE! ALL READY TO FRY! WHAT DO YOU SAY, MIKE?

COULD I HAVE A HOT DOG?

I'M FINE, MOM, I'M HAVING A GREAT TIME!

WE WENT FISHING, WE WENT TO THE ZOO AN' THE BEACH AN' THE WATER SLIDES...

...GRANDMA AN' I ARE GOING TO THE PLANETARIUM TOMORROW— AN' THEN WE'RE GOING OUT TO DINNER...

CAN I STAY HERE FOREVER?!!

WHEN'S MICHAEL COMING HOME?

IN A FEW DAYS.

WHEN? HUH? WHEN'S HE COMING HOME?

SOON!

WHY DO YOU KEEP ASKING THE SAME QUESTION, ELIZABETH!?

...CAUSE IT ISN'T THE SAME WIFOUT HIM.

THERE, THAT'S A GOOD JOB WELL DONE!

WITH MICHAEL AWAY, I'VE BEEN ABLE TO CLEAN OUT HIS ENTIRE ROOM!

HE'LL NEVER MISS ALL THE JUNK I'VE THROWN OUT. BESIDES.... WHO'S GOING TO TELL HIM?

YOU'VE BEEN AWAY QUITE A WHILE NOW, MICHAEL. ARE YOU GETTING A LITTLE HOMESICK?

UM...MAYBE... I DON'T THINK I MISS HOME SO MUCH—

...JUST THE PEOPLE IN IT.

WHAT'S TAKING MICHAEL SO LONG?

GIFT GALLERY

HE'S BUYING PRESENTS TO TAKE TO EVERYONE BACK HOME.

HOW SWEET! WAS IT HIS OWN IDEA?

YEP. IT WASN'T HIS OWN MONEY, BUT IT WAS HIS OWN IDEA.

WHERE'S GRANDMA!? EVERY TIME I'M READY TO GO SOMEWHERE— SHE STARTS PUTTERING AROUND!

FOR 36 YEARS WE'VE BEEN MARRIED—AND FOR 36 YEARS SHE'S DONE THE SAME DARNED THING!

WANT ME TO GO INSIDE AN' ASK HER TO HURRY UP, GRAMPA?

WHAT, AND RUIN A TRADITION?

ANYONE SEEING A LITTLE GIRL AGE 4, WEARING A YELLOW T-SHIRT...

LAST SEEN ON ARRIVALS FLOOR ...ANSWERING TO THE NAME OF ELIZABETH PATTERSON...

PHOTOS 50¢

LISTEN, BUNNY—SOMEONE HERE GOTS THE SAME NAME AS ME!!

AIR CANADA FLIGHT 119 FROM VANCOUVER IS NOW ARRIVING AT GATE-

AAAGH! THAT'S MY SON'S PLANE—AND ELIZABETH IS STILL MISSING!

GO MEET YOUR PLANE, MA'AM, WE'LL FIND HER —DON'T WORRY.

SECURITY

I'M NOT WORRIED... I'M **HYSTERICAL!**

MOM? MOM! WHERE'S MOM?!

WHAT'S THE MATTER, DEAR? WHERE'S YOUR MOMMY?

I DUNNO!!

I WEN' IN DERE TO SIT DOWN... AN' WHEN I CAME OUT—

SHE WAS **LOST!**

LICK! SLURP- LICK- OOH! UGH!

CUT IT OUT, FARLEY— STOP LICKING ME!

YOU'VE BEEN AWAY SO LONG— HE'S JUST HAPPY TO SEE YOU!

YEAH! MAYBE HE FORGOTS WHAT FLAVOR YOU ARE!

MOM THREW OUT YOUR OL' BATMAN CAPE WHILE YOU WERE GONE, MICHAEL..

SHE THREW OUT A RED CAR, A PAINT SET, SOME CHALK, SOME COMICS, LOTSA PAPER..

AAAGH!!! NOT MY PAINTS! NOT MY CAPE! LEMME SEE!

MOM WAS WRONG! SHE SAID HE'D NEVER NOTICE!

TOY CHEST

THE THINGS I THREW OUT OF YOUR ROOM WERE BROKEN, RUSTY AND OLD, MICHAEL.

BUT THEY WERE MINE! YOU CAN'T THROW OUT MY STUFF WITHOUT ASKING ME FIRST!

AND I SAY IF YOU REALLY WANTED THOSE THINGS, YOU'D HAVE LOOKED AFTER THEM IN THE FIRST PLACE!

I DID LOOK AFTER THEM! I KEPT THEM, DIDN'T I?

WHAT'S GOING ON HERE? MICHAEL'S ONLY JUST COME HOME AND THERE'S TROUBLE ALREADY!

WE'RE A FAMILY AGAIN! WE LOVE EACH OTHER!

NOW—WHAT'S THE POINT IN CONTINUING THIS ARGUMENT?

I WAS WINNING!!

MICHAEL, YOU'RE FILTHY! WHERE HAVE YOU BEEN!?

GORDON'S DAD TOOK US TO THE DUMP TO SEE IF WE COULD FIND MY STUFF YOU THREW OUT.

WE LOOKED ALL OVER. BUT WE COULDN'T FIND IT.

SO I BROUGHT HOME SOMEBODY ELSE'S STUFF INSTEAD!

CAN YOU BELIEVE IT? SOMEBODY ACTUALLY THREW OUT THIS PLASTIC BASEBALL BAT!

IT'S SPLIT DOWN THE SIDE. YOU COULD FILL IT FULL OF JUNK AN' SWING IT AROUND!

THERE'S SO MUCH NEAT STUFF AT THE DUMP. I'D LOVE TO WORK THERE WHEN I GROW UP!

'COURSE—MOM'D WANT ME TO GO TO UNIVERSITY FIRST.

SO... WHAT'S YOUR NEW TEACHER LIKE?

I DUNNO. IT'S SORTA HARD TO TELL THE FIRST DAY.

SOMETIMES THEY START OUT REAL MEAN, BUT TURN OUT TO BE NICE...AN' SOMETIMES THEY START OUT NICE — BUT TURN OUT TO BE MEAN.

...I THINK THIS ONE'S OF THE FIRST VARIETY.

MICHAEL—AREN'T YOU DRESSED YET? DON'T EAT THE TOOTHPASTE, LIZZIE! GET YOUR SOCKS ON! WHERE'S YOUR SWEATER? HURRY UP!!

AAGH! I CAN'T STAND THIS. I WISH THEY WERE STILL JUST SLEEPING IN!

BUT, ELLY — YOU COULDN'T WAIT FOR SCHOOL TO START SO YOU COULD GET BACK TO A ROUTINE!

I KNOW. I'D FORGOTTEN THE ROUTINE.

MICHAEL, I PUT THIS CLEAN, IRONED PILE OF CLOTHES HERE FOR YOU TO PUT AWAY AND LOOK AT THEM!!

THEY'RE A MESS!!

DON'T EXPECT ME TO FOLD THEM AGAIN. YOU CAN JUST LOOK LIKE A SLOB!

THE WORD IS "CASUAL".

"GRUMBLE))" ...HERE I AM FOLDING ALL MICHAEL'S CLOTHES AGAIN!!

HE JUST PULLS STUFF OUT... DOESN'T CARE ABOUT ANYTHING...

WHEN IS HE GOING TO START KEEPING HIS *!G DRAWERS TIDY?!!

...WHY DON'T YOU LEAVE THAT FOR HIS WIFE TO WORRY ABOUT!

I WASN'T CUT OUT FOR HOUSEWORK JOHN. THERE'S NOTHING I HATE MORE THAN CLEANING AND PICKING UP AFTER OTHER PEOPLE.

WHY IS IT ALWAYS UP TO ME TO KEEP THIS PLACE SHOVELED OUT?!

SOMEBODY HAS TO DO IT!!

BOY, MOM SURE IS A GROUCH TODAY.... WHAT'S BUGGING HER?

IT'S HORMONES, MIKE. SOMETHING PECULIAR TO WOMEN. MAKES 'EM MOODY FROM TIME TO TIME.

I HEARD THAT! THERE'S NOTHING WRONG WITH ME. I'M JUST SICK OF PICKING UP AFTER *YOU!*

I SEE WHAT YOU MEAN.

YOU'RE RIGHT, JOHN— IT'S HORMONES.

ELLY'S GETTING ON IN YEARS. SHE'S OVER 35. SHE COULD BE HEADING INTO THE "CHANGE OF LIFE".

HAVE YOU NOTICED ANY RADICAL MOOD SWINGS?

YEAH...

BUT IT'S MORE LIKE A STRONG LEFT HOOK!

THERE'S NOTHING WRONG WITH ME, JOHN! IT'S JUST HARD FOR ME TO BE NEEDED IN TWO PLACES AT ONCE!

I GO TO WORK—AND WORK LIKE CRAZY—THEN I COME HOME AND WORK LIKE CRAZY. IT'S STARTING TO GET ME DOWN!

IF IT'S TOO MUCH FOR YOU, ELLY.....WHY DON'T YOU QUIT THE JOB?

WHICH ONE?

ALL RIGHT, EVERYBODY. HEAR THIS!! THERE WILL BE NO SUPPER UNTIL THIS PLACE IS CLEANED UP—AND I MEAN **CLEANED!**

THIS IS WORK TO RULE !!

WHAT DOES "WORK TO RULE" MEAN?

WE WORK— SHE RULES.

LIZZIE AN' I CLEANED UP OUR WHOLE ROOMS, MOM. WANNA SEE?

WONDERFUL, MICHAEL! MUCH BETTER.

WITHOUT ALL THE JUNK AND CLUTTER— YOU CAN HAVE SOME _PRIDE_ IN YOUR ROOM!

...I SORTA HAD PRIDE IN THE JUNK AND CLUTTER.

YEAH, WHEN MY MOM WENT BACK TO WORK, WE HAD TO START DOING HOUSE—WORK TOO.

HECK—I EVEN DID THE LAUNDRY ONCE!

ONCE? HOW COME YOU ONLY HAD TO DO IT ONCE?

I DID IT WRONG.

...NOW...I PUT THE KNIFE AN' FORK INNA GLASS LIKE DIS...

ELIZABETH!! THAT'S NO WAY TO SET A TABLE!

OH. YEAH.

I FORGOT PLATES!

YEAH, MOM. I FINALLY GOT THE KIDS TO START PITCHING IN AROUND HERE AND PICK UP AFTER THEM-SELVES!

OH, IT TOOK SOME TIME. I HAD TO FIGHT ...I HAD TO THREATEN — BUT I DID IT!

RIGHT...UH HUH...OVER ONE HURDLE AND ONTO THE NEXT.

SO... WE'VE MADE A DEAL. HE HELPS OUT WITH THE HOUSEWORK ON THE DAYS I WORK...

...AND I TAKE CARE OF IT ON THE DAYS I'M HOME.
SOUNDS GOOD TO ME!

WHAT KIND OF FEMINIST LOGIC DID YOU USE ON HIM THIS TIME?

I CRIED.

MOM, I GOT LIZZIE ALL DRESSED UP FOR HALLOWEEN, AN' YOU GOTTA GUESS WHAT SHE IS!

HMM. IS SHE A CLOWN? NOPE. LITTLE RED RIDING HOOD? NOPE. A LITTLE GHOSTIE? NOPE. A BALLERINA? NOPE.

OK, I GIVE UP. WHAT IS SHE?

A PUNK ROCKER!!

AW, COME ON, MOM— SHE WANTS TO BE A PUNK ROCKER FOR HALLOWEEN, DON'T YOU, LIZ!

HEY, SHOW MOM SOME MEAN FACES! YEAH—NOW ACT ALL COOL LIKE!

MICHAEL, THAT LOOKS ABSOLUTELY AWFUL!

IT DOES?

KID, YOU'RE DOING GREAT!

ELIZABETH—A PUNK ROCKER, OF ALL THINGS!

ALL THE KIDS LIKE TO DRESS UP AS VIDEO STARS, EL! IT'S ONLY A COSTUME!

HECK, IT DOESN'T FAZE ME ONE BIT!

GOOD. MICHAEL WANTS TO BE BOY GEORGE.

WOW, MAN! LOOKIT THIS! THEY'RE GONNA BE SHOWIN' SCARY FLICKS ON CHANNEL 5 ALL NEXT WEEK!

WOULDN'T IT BE NEAT IF "GREMLINS" WAS ON?

YEAH! GROSS! 'MEMBER THE GUY BLOWS UP IN THE MICROWAVE? YEAH! EVER SICK! YOU SAW GUTS AN' EVERYTHING!

SIGH...ooo WHAT EVER HAPPENED TO "THE SOUND OF MUSIC?"

HEY, GUYS, MAYBE WE COULD HAVE A HALLOWEEN PARTY AT SOMEBODY'S HOUSE THIS YEAR!

YEAH! SOMEBODY COULD RENT SOME VIDEOS AND WE COULD DRESS UP AN' STUFF!

SOMEBODY COULD GET SOME FOOD, AN' SOME POP — WHADDYA THINK, MIKE?

GREAT!

I'LL GO ASK SOMEBODY.

A HALLOWEEN PARTY? HERE? BUT MIKE, OUT OF 6 FRIENDS, SURELY THERE'S SOMEONE ELSE'S MOTHER YOU COULD ASK!

AW, MOM! 'COURSE NOT!

THEIR MOMS ARE ALL BUSY!!

IT'S HARD BEING THE YOUNGEST, ISN'T IT, LIZ? THE BIG KIDS JUST DON'T WANT YOU AROUND.

BUT I THINK YOU'RE JUST FINE! AND I WANT YOU AROUND—SO THERE.

DADDY?

UH HUH.

I GOT SOMEFING FOR YOU.

THIS!!

MOM? MOM! CAN YOU HELP ME, PLEASE? MOM? MOMMY! MOM, I CAN'T DO THIS—YOU DO IT! CUT IT FOR ME! HELP ME, MOM! MOMMY! MOM! MOM?

THERE!!

BOY! ISN'T IT A GOOD THING DAD SAID WE COULD EACH DO OUR OWN PUMPKIN!!

BOY, THE AIR SMELLS FRESH TODAY. AN' THE LEAVES ARE REALLY FALLING!

DON'TCHA JUST LOVE THE COLORS, DADDY? DON'TCHA JUST LOVE THE WAY THEY CRUNCH? DON'TCHA JUST LOVE THIS TIME OF YEAR?

YEAH. HEAPS.

HOW COME YOUR MOM WOULDN'T LET YOU GUYS DRESS UP LIKE PUNK ROCKERS LAST NIGHT?

BOY... AN' I THOUGHT YOUR MOM WAS REAL COOL, MAN.

IT'S JUST CHAINS AN' MAKEUP AN' STUFF. SO WHAT IF SOME GUYS PUT SAFETY PINS THROUGH THEIR NOSES!

YEAH! IT'S JUST FOR FUN!

OH, MAYBE I'M BEING OVER-PROTECTIVE, ANNE.

I JUST COULDN'T SEE MY INNOCENT LITTLE KIDS ALL DRESSED UP IN LEATHER AND BIZARRE MAKEUP!

IN OUR DAY, IT WAS "MAKE LOVE, NOT WAR." WHY ARE THE KIDS TODAY SO ANGRY?!

MAYBE IT'S BECAUSE WE'RE CLOSER TO MAKING WAR.

OK! ALL RIGHT!! SOMEBODY'S BEEN STEALING MY CANDY!

I'M MISSING A WHOOPEE BAR, TWO RED-HOTS, A LICORICE WHIP — AN' AT LEAST SEVEN CARAMELS!

I THOUGHT I'D HELP YOU OUT, MIKE! YOU HAD SO MUCH, I THOUGHT...

YOU THOUGHT I COULDN'T KEEP TRACK.

WHAT AM I GOING TO DO WITHOUT HER? JEAN'S BEEN MY DENTAL ASSISTANT FOR YEARS!

SHE'S NOT GOING FOR A WHILE, JOHN. YOU HAVE TIME TO TRAIN SOMEONE ELSE.

YOU CAN'T REPLACE SOMEONE LIKE JEAN, ELLY. IT'D BE EASIER TO REPLACE A WIFE!

UH... FIGURATIVELY SPEAKING, THAT IS.

DON'T BE SILLY, JOHN! HOW CAN MY BEING PREGNANT AFFECT MY WORK?

I JUST PLAN TO USE THE LEAD APRON AND SHIELD WHEN I DO X-RAYS FROM NOW ON, THAT'S ALL!

UH... THIS LEAD IS A LITTLE HEAVY. COULD YOU PUSH ME TOWARD THE PATIENT, DOC?

I HAVE 7 APPLICATIONS FOR JEAN'S JOB ALREADY, EL. HOW AM I GOING TO CHOOSE ONE OUT OF ALL THESE PEOPLE?

WELL... CHUCK THIS ONE, IT'S FULL OF SPELLING MISTAKES. FORGET THIS ONE, IT'S WRITTEN IN PENCIL....

THIS ONE'S OUT! SHE'S WRITTEN ON PERFUMED PAPER AND TOLD YOU HER MEASUREMENTS!

LEMME SEE THAT!!

WHAT'S THE MATTER, MIKE?

THE WHOLE CLASS HAD TO STAY IN AFTER SCHOOL, THAT'S ALL!

AN' WE WEREN'T EVEN DOING ANYTHING! IT'S NO FAIR! A WHOLE CLASS GETS PUNISHED FOR NO REASON!

WE WEREN'T DOING A THING! ...ONE BURP AN' ONE SPITBALL AN' THE WHOLE CLASS....

I KNEW THERE WAS ANOTHER SIDE TO THE STORY.

WHAT'S FOR SUPPER, MOM?

"WAIT-AND-SEE PUDDING"!

THAT'S WHAT MY GRANDMA WOULD SAY WHENEVER WE ASKED HER THAT QUESTION!

DID MOM SAY WHAT WE'RE HAVIN' FOR SUPPER?

YEAH.

LEFTOVERS.

YOU GONNA HIRE SOMEBODY REAL PRETTY TO BE YOUR NEW ASSISTANT, DADDY?

MICHAEL, DECISIONS LIKE THAT AREN'T BASED ON LOOKS! WE INTERVIEW EVERYONE SERIOUSLY.

MY STAFF AND I HAVE TO CONSIDER THEIR QUALIFICATIONS, EXPERIENCE, ATTITUDE, ABILITY AND REFERENCES....

...THEN WE HIRE THE ONE YOUR MOTHER LIKES.

FARLEY WON'T EAT HIS SUPPER AGAIN, MOM, HE WANTS PEOPLE FOOD!

NO, MICHAEL. IF YOU LET HIM HAVE WHAT WE'RE EATING ALL THE TIME, HE'LL GET SPOILED.

ON THIS STUFF?

WHASSAT? SHHH.... I SNUCK FARLEY A WEENIE OUTA THE FRIDGE!

I'M TELLING! MOOOM! YOU SAID NOT TO FEED THE DOG, AN' MICHAEL JUST GIVED HIM A WEEENIE!!

YOU'RE A FINK, ELIZABETH. A DIRTY RAT FINK!

...JUST DOING MY JOB!

GO, MIKE! SKATE! GET IN THERE, BOYS! GO TEAM GO!! YAAAAAY!!

THAT'S IT, ELLY! TRYING TO KEEP UP THE TEAM SPIRIT!

ARE YOU KIDDING? I'M TRYING TO KEEP WARM!

WE GOTTA GET OUR-SELVES READY THIS YEAR, AN' WE GOTTA TIE OUR OWN SKATES!

NOW THAT I'M IN TOM THUMBS, NO MOMS ARE ALLOWED IN THE DRESSING ROOMS.

SORRY TO DISAPPOINT YOU, MOM, BUT YOU CAN'T COME IN HERE.

THESE SKATES DON'T FIT ME ANY-MORE, MOM. I'M GONNA NEED NEW ONES.

COACH SAYS I SHOULD GET THE LONG PANTS, TOO. THEY'RE ONLY ABOUT $90.

PLEASE, MOM? HOCKEY IS THE BEST THING IN MY WHOLE LIFE!!

WHO EVER SAID "THE BEST THINGS IN LIFE ARE FREE"?!!

LOOK, MOM! DADDY AN' I MADE A CAKE!

DADDY PUT THE STUFF INNA BOWL, AN' MIXED IT UP, AN' PUT IT INNA PAN AN' DEN INNA OVEN!

I THOUGHT YOU SAID YOU BOTH MADE THE CAKE, LIZZIE. WHAT DID YOU DO?

I HAD TO SHOW HIM WHERE EVERYTHING WAS!

WHAT— YOU'RE NOT FINISHED YET?!!

YOU HAVEN'T GOT YOUR 'JAMAS ON, YOU HAVEN'T DRIED YOUR HAIR... YOU HAVEN'T DONE YOUR TEETH...

WHAT DO I HAVE TO DO — COME UP HERE AND STAND OVER YOU?!

DUMB QUESTION.

WHY DO I HAFTA GO TO BED NOW? I GOT 10 MINUTES LEFT!

BECAUSE THIS IS THE FIRST TIME ALL WEEK THAT YOUR DAD AND I HAVE HAD A CHANCE TO SEE EACH OTHER.

I WANT US TO BE ALONE TOGETHER, LIKE AN OLD HAPPILY MARRIED COUPLE.

GZZNNNNN ZZZMMM

YOU — WERE DANCING TO "THRILLER"? WOW! GROSS-OUT!!

A BUNCH OF TUBBY LADIES DANCING AROUND TO MICHAEL JACKSON! I CAN'T STAND IT!!!

HI, HONEY... WHAT DID YOU DO AT DANCER-CISE TONIGHT?

DON'T ASK.

WITH ALL THAT EXERCISING, ELLY, YOU DON'T SEEM TO BE LOSING ANY WEIGHT.

WHAT?!!

WELL, FOR YOUR INFORMATION *!@* AND YOU CAN JUST *!@*Ø*!!!!

SORRY. I DIDN'T MEAN TO BE HONEST!

MICHAEL, I ASKED YOU AN HOUR AGO TO CLEAN UP YOUR ROOM.

I WILL.

...MICHAEL, CLEAN UP THIS ROOM!!

I'M GOING TO!

OUTER SPACE

MICHAEL, I —

HONEST, MOM... I AM GOING TO CLEAN UP MY ROOM!!

I KNOW. I JUST WANT IT DONE IN MY LIFETIME.

MOM'S HOME, DADDY. SHE WENT DOWN TO GET THE GROCERIES YOU LEFT AT THE STORE.

THEY'D PACKED EVERYTHING YOU HAD IN THE BASKET BEFORE THE ACCIDENT, JOHN. THEY WERE VERY CONCERNED.

HONEY... AS A GESTURE OF GOOD WILL, THEY GAVE US THE TURKEY THAT FELL ON YOUR FOOT.

SHALL WE EAT IT... OR HAVE IT BRONZED?

JEAN CAN'T COME IN TODAY, JOHN. SHE'S HAVING A BAD BOUT OF MORNING SICKNESS.

GREAT. I COME TO WORK WITH MY FOOT IN A CAST... AND NO ASSISTANT!

OH WELL, HERE GOES...

OPEN, PLEASE.

SPLAT!

WHY ME?

WHAT DO YOU MEAN "WHY YOU"?

DEP THE HOUSE WIF BALLS OF FOLLY-FALLA LA LA LAAH-LA LA NA NAAAAH!

YOU GOT ALL THE WORDS WRONG, DUMMY. IT'S DECK THE HALLS. DON'TCHA KNOW WHAT DECK MEANS?

BOP

... KID'S NOT AS DUMB AS SHE LOOKS.

WHERE'S DADDY?

HE'S TRYIN' TO HAVE A SHOWER WITH A BAG ON HIS FOOT.

IS HE COMING TO SEE YOUR CHRISTMAS PLAY?

I HOPE SO.

SILENT NIGHT HOLY NIGHT

I GET TO BE JOSEPH! MOM FOUND A NEAT COSTUME FOR ME AN' EVERY-THING!

ELLY!! HAS ANYONE SEEN MY BATH-ROBE?!

ISN'T THAT NICE, LIZZIE! I JUST LOVE THESE CHRISTMAS PLAYS.

I GET SO EMOTIONAL, I CRY.... IT'S SO EMBARRASSING!

I WISH I WERE AS MATTER-OF-FACT ABOUT THESE THINGS AS JOHN IS!

SNIFF!

YES, IT'S TRUE, MOM! JOHN DROPPED A FROZEN TURKEY ON HIS FOOT. UH-HUH, CAST, CRUTCHES, THE WHOLE WORKS!

AND THE SUPERMARKET GAVE US THE TURKEY — ISN'T THAT A RIOT? NOW, WHAT AM I GOING TO DO WITH A 25-LB. TURKEY?!!!

ELLY?!!

STUFF IT!!!

THE KIDS ARE ASLEEP ALREADY? THAT'S AMAZING!

YEAH... I REMEMBER WHEN I WAS THEIR AGE LYING AWAKE... TOO EXCITED ABOUT SANTA TO EVEN THINK ABOUT SLEEPING!

ME, TOO. I COULD NEVER SLEEP ON CHRISTMAS EVE WHEN I WAS LITTLE.

HEH, HEH... WELL, G'NIGHT, HONEY.

I CAN'T SLEEP.

...FOR WHAT WE ARE ABOUT TO RECEIVE, MAY THE LORD MAKE US TRULY....

POW! KA-BLAM!! WHADDYA THINK OF THE NEAT GUN AUNTIE MAVIS SENT ME!?

I DON'T LIKE GUNS, MIKE. AND I FEEL UNCOMFORTABLE AROUND PEOPLE WHO DO.

BUT IT'S PRETEND. SEE?!

I DON'T CARE!

AW, MOM! YOU GOT ABSOLUTELY NO IMAGINATION!

HAPPY NEW YEAR!!! SHOULD OLD ACQUAINTANCE BEEE FORGOT AND....

SO... WHAT ARE YOUR NEW YEAR'S RESOLUTIONS, PHIL?

I'M NOT TELLING YOU!

WHY NOT?!

YOU'D MAKE ME KEEP THEM!!

MOM AN' DAD ARE STILL SLEEPING!

BOY, THIS PLACE IS A MESS!

PEOPLE EVEN FORGOT TO FINISH THEIR DRINKS.

TO YOU, MY DEAR!

YOU TRY SOME FIRST AN' TELL ME WHAT IT'S LIKE.

THAT GOOD, HUH.

CUT IT OUT! YOU'LL WAKE UP MOM AN' DAD!

FWEEEBLPPT!

I WANNA PLAY AROUND IN HERE BEFORE THEY GET UP!

WHAT IF MOM FINDS OUT YOU BEEN PLAYING WITH ALL THE LEFTOVER DRINKS?

DON'T BE STOOPID, LIZ! HOW'S SHE GONNA KNOW!?

ICK! ICK! ICK!

HEY, THERE'S A CIGAR HERE! SOMEBODY LEFT A WHOLE CIGAR!

YOU'RE NOT GONNA LIGHT IT?!

JUST ONE END.

AK!! SMELLS LIKE UNCLE DANNY'S PIG BARN! HOW COME ANYBODY WOULD SMOKE THOSE THINGS!?

I DUNNO. MAYBE THEY WANT TO BE NOTICED.

: SNIFF... SNIFF :

— I SMELL SOMETHING BURNING!

WAAAAAAAAAAAAAAAAAAAAAAAAAAAA

JOHN, WAKE UP!

OOH... GROAN! MMMM...

AAAAAAAAAAAAAAAAAAAA

MY HEAD... WON'T STOP RINGING...

AAAAAAAAAAAAA

IT'S NOT YOUR HEAD, DUMMY, IT'S THE SMOKE DETECTOR!

WHAT'S GOING ON!? WHAT'S HAPPENING?!

MICHAEL LIT A CIGAR AN' PUT IT INNA WASTE-BASKET AN' IT CAUGHT FIRE AN' THE ALARM WENT OFF AN' THEN YOU AN' MOM GOT UP!

WELCOME TO 1985.

77

CAN I HELP YOU, DADDY? CAN I TAKE YOUR COAT?

I WANNA HELP DADDY! I WAS GONNA HELP HIM!

IT'S SURE NICE OF YOU TWO TO WANT TO GIVE ME A HAND LIKE THIS!

YEAH! AS SOON AS YOU SIT DOWN, WE CAN PLAY WITH YOUR CRUTCHES!

HEY, THIS IS A NEAT MAGNIFYIN' GLASS YOU GOT FROM SANTA, LIZZIE!

NEAT! I CAN SEE ALL THE LITTLE KNOBS ON YOUR TONGUE! WOW! THERE'S MILLIONS OF 'EM!

GO SHOW MOM!

MICHAEL! DID YOU PUT HER UP TO THIS?!!

TURKEY AGAIN?!! BUT WE HAD IT LAST NIGHT AN' THE NIGHT BEFORE LAST!

WE'VE HAD TURKEY STUFFED, TURKEY STEW, TURKEY PIE, TURKEY ON BUNS, TURKEY SALAD....

AT LEAST I'M BEING CREATIVE! YOU'VE GOT TO ADMIT I'VE GIVEN YOU A VARIETY!

YEAH....DADDY'S BEEN CALLING YOU THE "LEFTOVER QUEEN."

JOHN, FARLEY WAS PICKED UP BY SOMEONE IN A BLUE VAN! A MAN IN THE NEXT BLOCK TOLD ME!

BLUE VAN?! WHO IN THE WORLD WOULD WANT TO PICK UP FARLEY?

HERE WE GO, TIM. NO LICENSE, NO COLLAR, NO NOTHING!

EASTGATE ANIMAL POUND

YES, MA'AM... I THINK WE MIGHT HAVE YOUR DOG HERE.

BIG, SHAGGY... ANSWERS TO "FARLEY", DOES HE.

SURE, SURE. YOU CAN COME AND PICK HIM UP.

.... BAIL IS POSTED AT 20 BUCKS.

THE CHARGE IS: RUNNING AT LARGE - AND WITHOUT A LICENSE.

YOU'RE LUCKY. THE CHAP WHO CALLED US WANTED TO INCLUDE WILLFUL DAMAGE TO PRIVATE PROPERTY.

WHAT? WHICH ONE OF OUR NEIGHBORS WOULD TURN IN FARLEY?!

CHECK THE ONE WITH THE SNOW SCULPTURE.

EASTGATE ANIMAL POUND

I DON'T KNOW WHY I NEVER GOT HIM A LICENSE JOHN. I JUST NEVER THOUGHT ABOUT IT.

YEAH! FARLEY HAD TO GO TO THE POUND 'CAUSE HE WAS CAUGHT WALKING DOWN THE STREET WITHOUT A LICENSE!

MOM?

YES, ELIZABETH?

YOU GOT A LICENSE FOR ME?!!

OOH... THIS CAST ITCHES. IT'S DRIVING ME CRAZY!

KNOCK! KNOCK!

I'M SICK OF SITTING! I'M SICK OF CRUTCHES! I'M SICK OF THE HASSLE!

I WANT TO GO OUT! I WANT TO GET THINGS DONE! I WANT TO BE BUSY!!

HI, JOHN! LAZING AROUND AGAIN, HMM?

I'M GLAD MICHAEL'S TAKEN AN INTEREST IN MUSIC, GEORGIA.

TA-TA-TAWAAAH.. TATTICA TAT-TAT....

YES. IT DOES A LOT TO DEVELOP ONE'S PERSONALITY!

YOU TOOK AN INTEREST IN THE ACCORDION WHEN YOU WERE A KID, DIDN'T YOU, ELLY?

YEAH.

...MOTHER SAID IT WOULD DEVELOP MY BUST.

GOOD GRIEF! LIZZIE'S FOUR..... I'VE FORGOTTEN HOW TO HANDLE A TWO-YEAR-OLD.

NO, NO, RICHARD! DIRTY! UCKY! DON'T TOUCH!

WANT COOKIE? NICE TOYS! DRINK GONE? GO POTTY!

AH, YES... THE RETURN OF THE TWO-WORD SENTENCE.

LOOK, LIZZIE! RICHARD IS HERE FOR A VISIT!

WOULD YOU WATCH HIM WHILE I START SUPPER?

UH HUH.

YOU WATCH HIM, NOW. ARE YOU SURE YOU CAN WATCH HIM?

UH HUH.

ARE YOU WATCHING HIM, ELIZABETH?

UH HUH.

MOM, BABY RICHARD'S PLAYING IN THE KITCHEN CUPBOARDS!

I KNOW. HE'S FINE, HONEY.

HE'S TAKEN ALL THE CANS OFF THE SHELVES.

I KNOW. HE'S FINE.

HE'S STACKING THEM UP IN PILES.

HE'S FINE.

AN' HE'S TAKEN ALL THE LABELS OFF 'EM.

HE'S *WHAT?!*

I DON'T KNOW WHERE ANNIE IS, SO I GUESS YOU'LL BE HAVING DINNER WITH US, KIDDO.

OH, WOW! I'LL GET THE HIGH CHAIR FROM THE CRAWL SPACE!

I'LL FIND THE BIBS AN' THE PLASTIC PLATES AN' THE BABY SPOONS!

SO. HOW DO YOU LIKE YOUR STEAK?

YA-GAH!!

SQUISH MUSH SMUSH SPLT

WELL, IT'S BEEN A LONG TIME SINCE WE HAD A BABY AT OUR TABLE!

YEAH! ISN'T HE NEAT?

SPLUSH MUSH

IT'S NOT VERY OFTEN WE HAVE A DINNER GUEST WHO MAKES US LOOK GOOD!

OH, ELLY — I'M SORRY TO HAVE BEEN SO LONG!

SINCE YOU HAD THE BABY I, UH .... DID SOME SHOPPING. YOU KNOW HOW IT IS!!

AREN'T YOU A LITTLE ANGRY, EL? SHE LEFT HIM AN AWFULLY LONG TIME.

OH. I GUESS NOT.

I KNOW HOW IT IS!

KNOW WHAT I'D LIKE TO GET ELLY FOR VALENTINE'S DAY, JEAN?

ONE OF THOSE GREAT BIG, FANCY, HEART-SHAPED BOXES OF CHOCOLATES!

IMAGINE ME BUYING HER SOMETHING AS SILLY AND SENTIMENTAL AS THAT!

...COULD YOU PICK ONE UP ON YOUR LUNCH HOUR?

MICHAEL, YOUR SCHOOL PARTY IS COMING UP. YOU'D BETTER GET ALL YOUR VALENTINES DONE!

I GOT TWO PACKAGES OF CARDS, THE NAMES OF ALL THE KIDS IN YOUR CLASS, AND A SPECIAL CARD FOR YOUR TEACHER.

THERE! ALL YOU HAVE TO DO IS SIT DOWN AND WRITE OUT EVERYBODY'S NAME.

SIGH.... EVERY YEAR I GOTTA GO TO ALL THIS TROUBLE!

HEY, THERE'S DEANNA, MIKE! FIRE ONE AT THE BACK OF HER HEAD! GO ON, DO IT, DO IT, DO IT!!

AWW-YOU'RE NOT GONNA DO IT, 'CAUSE YOU LIKE HER, DON'TCHA, MIKE! MICHAEL LOVES—

I DO NOT!!

THE DARNED THING'S STUCK TO THE FUZZ ON MY MITT.

DON'T WIGGLE THE CUTTER. WE WANT THE EDGES NICE AND SHARP!

THERE! NOW, WE CAN PUT THE SPRINKLES ON AND GET THEM INTO THE OVEN!

THESE ONES HAVE COOLED A LITTLE BIT, MOM. CAN I HAVE ONE NOW?

DADDY?... WOULD YOU LIKE A WARM HEART?

DO I HAFTA GO TO BED, MOM? I'M DRAWING A NEAT PICTURE!

HOW LONG WILL IT TAKE YOU TO FINISH?

I DUNNO.

DEPENDS ON HOW LONG DADDY SLEEPS.

STOMP CLUMP! STOMP CLUMP!

QUICK, LIZ, GET BACK TO YOUR OWN ROOM. DADDY'S COMING!!

GOOD NIGHT, MIKE.

NITE, NITE LIZZIE!

BOY, I WONDER HOW MANY DAYS WE GOT LEFT BEFORE HE GETS THAT CAST OFF!

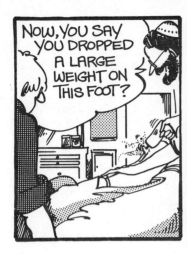

HAVE A TOUGH DAY, HONEY?

MY BEST ASSISTANT IS QUITTING, MY HYGIENIST IS SICK, I TRIED IN A BRIDGE THAT DIDN'T FIT, THEY SHUT THE WATER OFF AND MY FOOT IS KILLING ME!!

LEAVE DADDY ALONE, LIZ. HE'S IN A BAD MOOD.

WHEN CAN I TALK TO HIM?

WAIT 'TIL HIS EYES STOP BUGGING OUT.

WHAT'S YOUR NEW ASSISTANT'S NAME, DADDY?

LOUISE.

IS SHE NICE?

UH HUH.

IS SHE PRETTY?

UH HUH.

I ALWAYS HIRE PRETTY GIRLS, MIKE. GOTTA KEEP YOUR MOTHER ON HER TOES!

DADDY.... I THINK YOU JUST PUT YOUR FOOT IN YOUR MOUTH....

YOU KNOW I'M JUST KIDDING ABOUT THE GIRLS AT WORK, EL. I'M NOT INTERESTED IN ANYONE ELSE!

UH...HOW ABOUT YOU? DO YOU...HAVE YOU EVER... BEEN TEMPTED TO GO OUT LOOKING FOR OTHER ...MEN?

OF COURSE NOT!!

A NERD IN THE HAND IS WORTH TWO IN THE BUSH!

ELLY, I'M GLAD YOU'RE HERE. I WAS SUPPOSED TO GO TO WINNIPEG NEXT WEEK, BUT I CAN'T MAKE IT.

...COULD YOU ATTEND THIS WORKSHOP IN MY PLACE?

ME?!!!

PUPPETS WITH A PURPOSE

SUE, I'D HAVE TO GET SITTERS, ORGANIZE MY HOUSE, I COULDN'T POSSIBLY...

HERE ARE THE TICKETS, THE HOTEL IS TAKEN CARE OF.....

ME? TAKE OFF TO WINNIPEG JUST LIKE THAT? SUE, THEY'D THINK I WAS CRAZY!!!

...SPACIOUS HOTEL ROOM, A BATHROOM ALL TO YOURSELF, DINING OUT, NEW PEOPLE TO MEET, INTERESTING CONVERSATION... TIME... ALONE....

ELLY, ARE YOU REALLY GOING TO TURN THIS DOWN?

...I'D HAVE TO BE CRAZY!!!

I DON'T BELIEVE IT. THEY WANT ME TO GO ON A BUSINESS TRIP! ME!

BUT, WHAT WILL JOHN SAY? WHAT ABOUT HIM? WHAT ABOUT THE KIDS??

...I'D FEEL SO GUILTY ABOUT LEAVING THEM. I'D FEEL SO GUILTY... AND SO SELFISH...

FOR AN HOUR OR SO-AT LEAST!

I'M OFF TO A MEETING TO TRY AND GET A GOVERNMENT GRANT ARRANGED.

AND YOU?

I'M GOING TO A PUPPETRY WORKSHOP.

WELL... I SEE WE'RE BOTH INVOLVED IN SIMILAR PROJECTS THIS WEEK.

PULLING STRINGS!

WELL, IT'S BEEN A PLEASURE FLYING WITH YOU!

YES, THANKS FOR THE COMPANY!

DARN! I CAN'T FIND MY ITINERARY... I WISH I KNEW WHERE I WAS GOING!

DON'T WE ALL!

AAH... A HOTEL ROOM FOR TWO WHOLE NIGHTS!

NO COOKING, NO CLEANING, NO KIDS... JUST ME!

I HAVEN'T BEEN BY MYSELF FOR AGES AND AGES AND AGES!

HELLO, STRANGER.

KNOCK KNOCK

ROOM SERVICE!

UH?

OH, MY GOSH - I FORGOT TO SET MY ALARM!!

COULD YOU BRING THE TRAY BACK LATER, PLEASE? I'M NOT DRESSED! I LOOK AWFUL!

THAT'S OK, LADY. I'M USED TO IT.... I'M MARRIED.

HEH, HEH ... HELLO THERE, MRS ... UH ... PATTERSON!

NEARSIGHTED, MY FOOT!!

CLAIRE STANTON.

ELLY PATTERSON.

I DON'T KNOW A SOUL HERE, DO YOU?

NOT A SOUL.

I'M GOING TO SALON 'B'.

SO AM I — SHOULD WE SIT TOGETHER?

... I THINK I'M A PEOPLE WHO NEEDS PEOPLE.

WHAT DO I DO? ... LET'S SEE — I HELP WITH THE CHILDREN'S PROGRAMS AT OUR LIBRARY ....

I READ TO KIDS, TEACH CRAFTS, WORK WITH PERFORMERS, SHOW FILMS ...

I TAKE BOOKS TO THE HOSPITALS, I DO POSTERS, DISPLAYS, — I WRITE A LITTLE COLUMN FOR THE PAPER ...

— NOTHING SPECIAL.

I WORK WITH DIFFERENTLY ABLED KIDS. I THOUGHT THIS COURSE WOULD HELP ME TEACH READING TO THE YOUNG ONES.

SOUNDS LIKE A DIFFICULT JOB. — I MEAN ... TRYING TO TEACH KIDS THAT ARE ...

ARE YOU KIDDING? — THEY'RE ALL SMARTER THAN I AM !!

EXCUSE ME!

UH.... MISS? EXCUSE ME!

IS IT MY IMAGINATION..... OR ARE WE BEING IGNORED?

EXCUSE ME—COULD WE HAVE SOME CREAM FOR OUR COFFEE, PLEASE?

THUMP

WELL...ONE THING'S CERTAIN .... IF WE WANT THE WORLD TO TREAT WOMEN WITH RESPECT...

WE'RE GOING TO HAVE TO CHANGE THE WAY WE TREAT EACH OTHER!

WELL...THE SERVICE WAS TERRIBLE—OUR WAITRESS WAS RUDE...

THE COFFEE WAS COLD, WE HAD NO CREAM, WE ASKED FOR THE CHECK THREE TIMES...

I DON'T KNOW WHEN I'VE HAD A MORE UNPLEASANT MEAL.

RIGHT!

... SHOULD WE LEAVE A TIP?

I TALKED TO MY KIDS ON THE PHONE LAST NIGHT – THEY SURE MISS ME!

ELLY, YOU'VE ONLY BEEN AWAY TWO DAYS! DON'T GO FEELING GUILTY ALREADY!

CLAIRE – I'D FEEL GUILTY NO MATTER HOW LONG I WAS AWAY!

SO – NEXT TIME TAKE TWO WEEKS!

MY KIDS WOULD HAVE LOVED THAT LAST WORKSHOP! WE'D HAVE HAD TO DRAG THEM AWAY!

MINE TOO. THEY WOULD HAVE GONE CRAZY! – ABSOLUTELY WILD!!

THEY WOULD HAVE BEEN SO EXCITED ABOUT THE MUSIC, THEY WOULDN'T HAVE BEEN ABLE TO SIT STILL!

YEAH! .... IT'S A GOOD THING THEY'RE NOT HERE.

THAT WAS OUR LAST LECTURE, CLAIRE. IT'S OUR LAST NIGHT HERE – OUR LAST NIGHT OF FREEDOM.

SHOULD WE CELEBRATE?

DEFINITELY!

TO US! TO WOMEN! TO FRIENDSHIP!!

HAPPENS EVERY TIME YOU LET 'EM OUT OF THE KITCHEN, FRANK.

NOW... LET'S SEE... I'VE BOUGHT STUFF FOR THE KIDS, SOME CLOTHES FOR JOHN....

I VISITED HIS FOLKS, HIS SISTER AND TWO OF MY RELATIVES....

IF I RUSH, I CAN GET IN SOME MORE SHOPPING BEFORE I LEAVE FOR THE PLANE!

12.24

THESE BUSINESS TRIPS SURE ARE EXHAUSTING!

SALE

NOW. HOW AM I GOING TO GET ALL THIS STUFF INTO MY SUITCASE?

UGH! GRUNT... MMPH!!

AAAH!!

CLICK!

'SCUSE ME, MA'AM—YOU'VE LEFT A SKIRT, SOME SHOES AND TWO BLOUSES IN THE CLOSET!

MOM'S COMING HOME! MOM'S COMING HOME!!

SETTLE DOWN! GET YOUR JACKETS ON! STOP JUMPING AROUND!

CUT IT OUT! LEAVE THE DOG! GET YOUR SHOES! HURRY UP!!

MOM'S COMING HOME! MOM'S COMING HOME!!

THERE SHE IS! MOM'S HOME! SHE'S HERE!

KNOW WHAT, MOM? KNOW WHAT?

WHAT, HONEY?

EVEN IF YOU BROUGHT ME SOMETHING ... I'M NOT GONNA ASK IF YOU BROUGHT ME SOMETHING!

IT WAS A WONDERFUL TRIP, JOHN! THE COURSE WAS SUPER, I LEARNED A LOT, I MET SOME FANTASTIC PEOPLE ...

I LOVED BEING ON MY OWN, IT DID ME A WORLD OF GOOD!

I'LL HAVE TO GO AWAY MORE OFTEN !!

GUESS WHAT, MOM! WE GOT SOMETHING TO SHOW YOU!

NO, LIZZIE! SHHHH...

WE DID IT ALL BY OURSELVES – AN' YOU'RE GONNA LOVE IT !!

NO! YOU'RE GONNA SPOIL...

WE CLEANED UP THE HOUSE ALL BY OUR- AAAAAAAH!!

YOU DUMMY, ELIZABETH! I WANTED HER TO BE SURPRISED!

SEE? I TOLD YOU! WE TIDIED UP THE WHOLE HOUSE FOR YOU, MOM!

WE PICKED UP OUR STUFF, AN' MADE OUR BEDS, AN' MICHAEL EVEN WASHED THE KITCHEN FLOOR!

YOU WASHED THE FLOOR?

I SORT OF HAD TO.

...LIZZIE DID THE DISHES.

WHILE YOU WERE AWAY, DADDY SHOWED US HOW TO COOK!

IT WAS EASY! WE HAD PEAS, AN' 'TATOES, AN' CHICKEN AN' EVERYTHING!

DADDY SHOWED YOU HOW TO COOK ALL THOSE THINGS?

YEAH! JUST PUT ONE OF THESE IN THE OVEN — AN' TURN IT UP TO 450°!

Stingios DELUXE T.V. DINNER

I MISSED YOU, EL.

I MISSED YOU, TOO.

ONE GOOD THING ABOUT TRAVELING ALONE IS... YOU GET TO MEET A LOT OF NEW PEOPLE.

DID YOU COMPARE ME TO ANYBODY?

SURE!

...HOW DID I DO?

NO COMPARISON!

CAN'T MIKE AN' LAWRENCE COME IN, MOM?

NO. I TOLD THEM YOU ALREADY HAD TWO FRIENDS IN, AND THAT'S ENOUGH.

THEY CAN'T COME IN?

NO.

OH. ...THAT'S TOO BAD.

NA-NA NA-NAAAA NAH!

MAAAH! LIZZIE'S MAKIN' FACES AT US THROUGH THE WINDOW!

MICHAEL, YOU'RE TOO OLD TO LET A 4-YEAR-OLD GET THE BEST OF YOU!

I'M NOT LETTIN' HER GET THE BEST OF ME!

—THIS IS THE WORST OF ME!!

WHAT'S THE MATTER, EL?

THE KIDS BOTH HAD FRIENDS OVER TODAY, AND I SPENT ALL MY TIME WIPING NOSES AND BEING REFEREE!

THEY WERE UNDER-FOOT ALL DAY DRIVING ME CRAZY. WHY DO I DO THIS TO MYSELF?!!

BECAUSE...IN A FEW YEARS THEY'LL DRIVE YOU CRAZY WONDERING WHERE THEY ARE!

WHAT? YOU HAVEN'T FINISHED THE GARAGE!?

IT'S TOO MUCH WORK!

MICHAEL, YOU DON'T KNOW WHAT WORK IS!!

I DO SO!

....THAT'S WHY I NEVER FINISHED THE GARAGE!

WOW, I DID IT! I MADE ENOUGH DOUGH TO BUY 3 SUPER-KOMIX AN' A WHOOPEE BAR!

BUT MIKE, I THOUGHT YOU WERE EARNING MONEY TO BUY MOM A MOTHER'S DAY GIFT!

MOTHER'S DAY?!

UH HUH.

CAN I BUY HER SOMETHIN' WITH THE CHANGE?

MOTHER'S DAY! I FORGOT ALL ABOUT IT! ...DO I HAFTA SPEND MY MONEY ON MOM?

NOPE.

YOU CAN EITHER SPEND IT SELFISHLY ON YOURSELF....

OR YOU CAN BUY SOMETHING NICE FOR SOMEONE WHO DOES A LOT OF NICE THINGS FOR YOU.

TAKE YOUR PICK!

HEY, LOOK AT THAT! THE CAKE RAFFLE IS TODAY!

HOME ECONOMICS CAKE RAFFLE TODAY 25¢ PER TICKET OR 5 FOR A DOLLAR

AREN'T YOU GONNA GET SOME TICKETS?

NAH. I WENT AN' FORGOT MY MONEY.

...WELL, I GUESS I COULD GIVE YOU ONE OF MINE — ON ONE CONDITION...

—YOU GOTTA GIVE IT BACK IF IT WINS!

QUIET, EVERYONE... WE'RE GOING TO DRAW THE WINNING NUMBER FOR THIS WEEK'S CAKE RAFFLE.

I CAN'T WAIT— IT'S CHOCOLATE FUDGE THIS TIME!

READY? THIS WEEK'S LUCKY NUMBER IS ... 661!!

GASP!

CONGRATULATIONS, BRAD LUGGSWORTH!

I DON'T BELIEVE IT! I JUST DON'T BELIEVE IT!

WHAT'S THAT, MIKE?

EVERY WEEK WE HAVE A CAKE RAFFLE AT SCHOOL—AN' THIS WEEK BRAD LUGGSWORTH WON!

HE'S STUPID AN' HE'S MEAN — EVERYBODY HATES HIM — WHY HIM? WHY DID IT HAFTA BE HIM?!

BECAUSE, MIKE... SOMETIMES A LOSER REALLY NEEDS TO WIN.

JOHN... COULD YOU HELP ME GET THIS BATHING SUIT ON?

MMMM MMHH

WHEW! THANKS.

IT WAS NOTHING...

SORT OF LIKE PUTTING SHEETS ON A WATER BED!

(GROAN) I LOOK AWFUL! I CAN'T GO OUT ONTO A BEACH LIKE THIS!

WHY NOT, FOR HEAVEN'S SAKE? YOU'RE OVER 35, YOU'VE HAD TWO KIDS... YOU'RE ENTITLED TO SPORT A FEW EXTRA ROLLS!

ACCEPT THE FACT THAT YOU'RE A LITTLE CHUNKY AND...

—SO MUCH FOR HONESTY IN MARRIAGE.

SO, HE SAYS TO ME, "ACCEPT THE FACT THAT YOU'RE A LITTLE CHUNKY!"

I'M TELLING YOU, ANNIE, I WAS SO MAD!!!

IF ONLY I COULD LOSE 10 LBS. I'D....

...WHY DO THE SKINNY ONES COME TO ME FOR SYMPATHY?!

WHAT'S FOR SUPPER?

ANNIE LENT ME HER CELEBRITY DIET COOKBOOK!

SEE... ALL THE RECIPES ARE BY FAMOUS PEOPLE!

WHAT'S IT CALLED, "SUFFER WITH THE STARS"?

JUST 'CAUSE YOU'RE ON A DIET, MOM, DO WE HAFTA EAT DIET FOOD?

SURE! IF I'M MAKING A SPECIAL MEAL, I MIGHT AS WELL MAKE IT FOR EVERYONE.

BESIDES, YOU'RE THE ONLY ONE WHO'S COMPLAINING. DADDY ISN'T SAYING ANYTHING!

THAT'S BECAUSE DADDY WANTS TO LIVE TO THE AGE OF RETIREMENT.

EAT YOUR YOGURT, ELIZABETH.

DON'T WANNA.

YOU SHOULD, LIZ— THERE'S BACTERIA IN IT, AN' IT'S REAL GOOD FOR YOU!

WHAT'S BAT-KEERIA?

LITTLE.... TINY.... BUGS.

JUST TRYING TO HELP!

UNH! UGH! GASP! ...THIS TREE MUST WEIGH 100 LBS.!!

'UNTIE SACKING, BURY ROOT BALL COMPLETELY, WATER WELL...'

WHAT DO YOU THINK, HONEY? LOOK OK'?

YEAH.

BUT I WANTED IT OVER THERE!

YOU KNOW THOSE FLOWERS YOU JUST PLANTED BY THE GARAGE, MOM?

UH HUH!

WHAT ARE THEY CALLED?

THEY'RE BEGONIAS, HONEY. WHY DO YOU WANT TO KNOW?

MICHAEL'S STANDING ON 'EM.

WHEW! GARDENING'S GOOD EXERCISE! I FEEL THINNER ALREADY!

LOOK AT ME, JOHN - DO I LOOK THINNER?

WELL?

WHAT CAN I SAY THAT WON'T GET ME INTO TROUBLE?

STEVE'S DOWNTOWN, ELLY, AND I'VE GOT THE CAR. COULD I LEAVE THE BOYS WITH YOU?..

WELL... I... UH....

THANKS, EL... I'LL ONLY BE AN HOUR OR SO.

I DON'T MIND TAKING THEM FOR AN HOUR.... IT'S THE "OR SO" THAT BOTHERS ME!

MICHAEL, HONEY... CHRIS AND LIZZIE ARE PLAYING NICELY DOWNSTAIRS...

WOULD YOU WATCH BABY RICHARD AND SEE THAT HE STAYS OUT OF TROUBLE?

BUT MOM, I'M DOIN' STUFF... AN' HE'S A REAL NUISANCE!!

BESIDES THAT.... HE'S NOT HOUSE-BROKEN.

HERE IT IS — I FOUND IT IN THE CRAWL SPACE!

BOY, GOOD THING YOU KEPT ALL OUR BABY JUNK. IT COMES IN HANDY!

COME ON, RICHARD, LET'S —

NO WAUNA!

MOM FORGOT TO TELL YOU — HE'LL ONLY GO ON HIS OWN POTTY.

JOHN, WOULD YOU GO NEXT DOOR AND GET RICHARD'S POTTY? I'M BABY-SITTING. AND IT'S THE ONLY ONE HE'LL USE!

PLEASE HURRY!

JOHN? WHAT'S TAKING SO LONG?

ANNIE LOCKED HER *!⊚✿ DOORS!!

ELLY, NO KID HAS TO HAVE HIS OWN POTTY! TELL HIM HE CAN—

BUT HE'S CRYING! CAN'T WE GET IN THROUGH A WINDOW?

BREAK INTO A HOUSE FOR A POTTY? ARE YOU CRAZY?!!

...SHE'S CRAZY!

OK, OK—THIS WINDOW SEEMS TO BE LOOSE. —THERE!

SHE KEEPS HIS POTTY IN THE LOWER HALL BATHROOM.

THIS IS RIDICULOUS. I HOPE NOBODY FINDS OUT I BROKE INTO A HOUSE FOR A...

RINGALINGA LINGA ALI RING ALING

122

GASP! IT'S A BURGLAR ALARM! JOHN'S SET OFF A BURGLAR ALARM!

GOOD GRIEF! HELP! IS THERE ANY WAY TO TURN THIS THING OFF?!!

IT'S OK, DAD — SOMEBODY'S COMING TO FIX EVERYTHING!

MRS. BAIRD'S CALLED THE POLICE!

ALARM TURN-OFF WAS IN THE CLOSET, SERGEANT.

NOW. YOU SAY YOU'RE A NEIGHBOR AND YOU GAINED FORCIBLE ENTRY TO THIS RESIDENCE TO GET A.... POTTY? ...IS THAT CORRECT?

YOU REALIZE THAT YOU COULD BE CHARGED WITH BREAKING AND ENTERING — AND THEFT?!!

THIS IS NEAT, MAN! JUST LIKE "MIAMI VICE"!

I DON'T BELIEVE THIS IS HAPPENING!

YOU CAN'T ARREST ME — I'M AN HONEST CITIZEN!

I'M A DENTIST!!!

I HATE DENTISTS!

HOLY COW, MIKE, IS YOUR DAD GOIN' TO JAIL?!!

NAH. HE JUST HASTA WAIT 'TILL ANNIE AN' STEVE GET HOME.

THEY HAFTA SIGN SOME PAPERS SAYIN' IT WAS OK THAT HE WAS IN THEIR HOUSE.

HONEST, HONEY, SHE SAID SHE'D BE RIGHT BACK!

MAMA! MAMA!

WHAT? JOHN BROKE INTO MY HOUSE? THE POLICE ARE HERE? OH, NO!

OH, NO!!!

ALL THOSE PEOPLE IN MY HOUSE...AND I NEVER DID MY DISHES OR ANYTHING!

ANNIE, YOU AND STEVE HAVE TO SIGN SOME FORMS SO THAT JOHN WON'T BE CHARGED WITH "BREAKING AND ENTERING."

HE BROKE IN TO GET A POTTY, MA'AM. I UNDERSTAND YOUR YOUNGEST NEEDS HIS OWN POTTY?.

YES, RICHARD CAN BE A HANDFUL!

...THE KID'S A *!G☆ BOATLOAD!

I'VE NEVER BEEN SO EMBARRASSED IN MY LIFE!

THE ENTIRE NEIGHBORHOOD WATCHED ME GET ARRESTED, FOR HEAVEN'S SAKE!

OH WELL... I GUESS SOME DAY WE'LL LOOK BACK AND LAUGH AT...

I SAID **SOME DAY!**

DADDY'S IN A BAD MOOD - SO I WANT YOU BOTH TO GET INTO YOUR P.J.'S AND INTO BED. NOW!

AWW!

LET'S GO, LIZZIE!

BUT I DON'T WANNA GO TO BED!

THE TROUBLE WITH YOU IS YOU DON'T LISTEN. SHE SAID GET INTO BED....

SHE NEVER SAID WE HAD TO SLEEP!

NEED A HUG, DADDY?

125